My Favorite

One Liners, Stories, Puns, Dad Jokes and Bad Jokes!

Whether you want to be the life of the party or just want a few jokes for your office workers, this book is for you. You can put together a few of these jokes and try stand up comedy! Long stories, short jokes, one liners and really bad puns make up this collection from the joke files of comedy magician and ventriloquist Bob Carroll.

 Bob is the author of The World's Most Famous Unknown Magician and Ventriloquist about his travels and magic tips for magicians. We hope that you will enjoy this collection of jokes.

Funny Business

Have you always wanted to be funny? Do you want to be the life of the party? Do you want to make people laugh? Well, if you answered yes, no or who cares to any of the questions, then you are on your way to making people laugh.

I have been a professional comic, magician and ventriloquist for over 50 years. Of course, I took time out for showers, food and sleeping. Do I know what is funny? Most of the time but comedy is subjective. What is hysterical to one person might offend another person. However, it is not up to me to decide who laughs at what joke. I just think these are funny, amusing and some stupid! There are some dad jokes, puns, quips, insults, one liners and just plain funny jokes in this collection. I don't claim that these jokes are all mine. I have collected these jokes over the years and am now sharing them with you.

In 1979, I told jokes for 24 hours and 5 minutes to get into the Guinness Book of Records. I memorized 8 hours of jokes and repeated it over and over. I do know a few jokes and will try to make you the life of the party in these pages. You will find these are funnier if you say them out loud to other people.

My number one fan is my wife Deb. If she thinks it is funny then that is all that matters to me. She has heard them all several times over. She still laughs at all of them. She is also my best critic. If the joke fails, she is the first to let me know that the joke needs work. The world needs to laugh so here are some corny, funny, punny, clever jokes!

So when I started posting all these jokes online over 5 years ago, people started asking me to put these all into a book. I decided not to put them into any specific category. When I read joke books, I like to be surprised at the humor but if you put them in categories, they become obvious. Use these jokes everywhere. If you are a comic, doctor, lawyer or funeral director, feel free to make people laugh. Enjoy!

Rest in Peace boiling water...You will be mist!

Three months ago, I paid $100 for the book "How to Scam Seniors" and it still hasn't arrived.

Everyone told Beethoven he could never be a great musician because he was deaf. But did he listen?

I must admit that you brought religion into my life because before I met you, I didn't know what Hell was.

What do you call an Italian astronaut? A specimen.

It's time to diet if your blood type is Ragu.

What do you call a hen who can count?
 A mathamachicken.
One bird can't make a pun. But toucan.

If you date a cross-eyed person, be careful.
They might be seeing other people on the
side.

I tied all of my spaghetti together when I
was drunk last night and ended up
skipping dinner.

My wife said, "You're so unromantic. I bet
you don't even know what my favorite
flower is."
"Is it Gold Medal?" I asked.

Photons have mass? I didn't even know
they were Catholic.

"One man's trash is another man's treasure"and that was the way they told me I was adopted

Possessio is nine tenths of the word.

The quickest way to call a family meeting is to turn off the WiFi and wait...

I've broken up with my gym.
Our relationship just wasn't "working out"

The Low Self Esteem Support Group will meet Thursday at 7 PM. Please use the back door.

My wife wanted a slow cooker. So I took 3 hours to make her an omelet.

A good limbo dancer lowers the bar for everyone else.

Last evening, I pulled an all nighter. I didn't wake up to pee til 8 am.

What do you call a person who doesn't know the difference between a spoon and a ladle? Fat.

My new car horn is the sound of screeching tires. I am going to have some fun with people on their phones in the crosswalk.

I don't have a tattoo but I do have a permanent stain on all my shirts.

The fact that Head and Shoulders doesn't have a body wash called Knees and Toes is crazy.

Where do the Easter Bunnies live?
All bunny, New York

After 75 years of research, scientists in Sweden have determined that no one has ever died from dirt behind the ears.

The snooze button inventor has passed away. His funeral will take place tomorrow at 10:00am, 10:09am, 10:18am, 10:27am...

Welcome to the Plastic Surgery Addicts group... I see a lot of new faces here today!

I like to hold hands at the movies... which always seems to startle the person next to me.

I will always remember where I was the day Facebook was down! Trying to get on Facebook.

A slug is really a snail who had his house taken away by the bank.

I don't care what that woodpecker says about me in Morse Code. I am not paranoid!

ARBITRATOR (ar'-bi-tray'-ter): A cook that leaves Arby's to work at Burger King.

AMNESIA: condition that enables a woman who has gone through labor to have sex again.

GRANDPARENTS: The people who think your children are wonderful even though they're sure you're not raising them right.

GROCERY LIST: What you spend half an hour writing, then forget to take with you to the store.

ABUNDANCE: a social event held at a bake shop.

I've learned that you cannot make someone love you. All you can do is stalk them and hope they panic and give in.

When you go into court you are putting yourself in the hands of 12 people that weren't smart enough to get out of jury duty.

What's the best restaurant on Tatooine? Pizza The Hutt!

Do you ever wonder about those people who spend $2.00 a piece on those little bottles of Evian water? Try spelling Evian backwards.

Why don't we ever see this headline: Psychic Wins Lottery ?

I am so old that I remember when there was only two commandments.

I am so old that I used to babysit Jesus.

I am so old that my social security number is 3.

Q: Why did Santa's helper see the doctor?
A: Because he had a low "elf" esteem!

Bill walks into a bar with a newt on his shoulder.

The barmaid looks at the creature and asks the man what he calls it.

'Tiny', answers Bill.

'Why's that?' asked the barmaid.

'Because he's my newt' says Bill.

A rubber band pistol was confiscated from algebra class because it was a weapon of math disruption.

An archaeologist is the best husband a woman can have.

The older she gets the more interested he is in her.

I just ate some Scrabble tiles by accident.

My next BM could spell disaster.

Wife: "Would you like an SUV for Christmas"
Husband: "Sure"
Wife: Ok, Socks, Underwear and Viagra it is!"

I am at the age where "if I get a little action" it means I don't need a laxative.

I like to sleep in the nude. I only wish the people on my flight were a little more understanding.

One of the most wonderful things in life is to wake up and enjoy a cuddle with somebody; unless you are in prison.

I wish the furniture store would quit calling me. I only wanted a one nightstand.

The past, present and future walk into a bar. It was tense.

I wonder what my parents did to fight boredom before the internet.
I asked my 16 brothers and sisters and they didn't know either.

A guy walks into a bar with a set of jumper cables.
The bartender says, buddy, I'll serve you as long as you don't start anything.

A skeleton walks into a bar and says give me a beer and a mop.

A grasshopper goes into a bar. The bartender says "We have a drink named after you." The grasshopper says "You have a drink named Irving?"

I go to the doctor complaining I'm a tepee I'm a wigwam, I'm a tepee I'm a wigwam. The doctor says "you know what your problem is, you're too tense."

I steal candy bars using sleight of hand. You could say I have a few Twix up my sleeve.

My friend thinks he is smart. He told me an onion is the only food that makes you cry, so I threw a coconut at his face.

A man came home to find his wife in bed with a stranger. "What the hell are you two doing?" He demanded. His wife turned to the stranger and said, "See, I told you he was stupid."

Charles Dickens walks into a bar and asks for a martini. The bartender asks, "Olive or twist?"

I am so old that when I go to the restaurant and order a three minute egg, they ask for the money up front.

After being married all these years, I just found out that my wife won't wake up and get me snacks at 7-11 at 3 AM.

I have always wanted to be a magician ever since I found out that the lady on the corner was making a $100 a trick!

How can you tell if your spouse has watched a lot of Dateline?
When you see a grocery list with rubber gloves, shovel, bleach, antifreeze.

My computer and I have a lot in common. If we don't have any activity in 30 minutes, we both go into sleep mode!

Whenever I find the key to success, someone changes the lock.

Whenever I fill out an application, in the part that says "If an emergency, notify:" I put "DOCTOR"

What's my wife going to do?

Don't you hate it when someone answers their own questions? I do.

I hate Russian dolls, they're so full of themselves.

I threw away a boomerang three years ago. Now I live in constant fear.

For Sale: Parachute. Only used once, never opened.

And the Lord said unto John. "Come forth and you will receive Eternal Life"
John came in fifth and won a toaster.

My wife told me I was acting very immature.
I told her to get out of my fort.

As I get older, I care less and less about a product that has a lifetime guarantee.

You know you are getting old when about half the stuff in your shopping cart says, "For fast relief"

People can be so gullible. For more information on this subject, please send me $20.

A stockbroker urged me to buy a stock that would triple its value every year. I told him at my age I don't even buy green bananas.

"An Apple A Day" is a good haul for a computer thief.

I own the erasers for all the miniature golf pencils.

When you are on trial, you are putting your fate into the hands of people who weren't smart enough to get out of jury duty.

Rejected greeting card: "I'm so miserable without you, it's almost like you're still here."

I discovered I scream the same way whether I'm about to be devoured by a great white shark or if a piece of seaweed touches my foot.

Thought of the day: Never, under any circumstances, take a sleeping pill and a laxative on the same night.

I saw a woman wearing a sweat shirt with "Guess" on it...so I said "Implants?"

Politicians and diapers have one thing in common. They should both be changed regularly, and for the same reason.

Honk if you love peace and quiet.

Question of the day. If quizzes are quizzical, what are tests?

Why don't sheep shrink when it rains?

I was reading in the paper today about this dwarf who had his pocket picked. How could anyone stoop so low?

A recent study has found that women who carry a little extra weight live longer than the men who mention it!

Why not put pictures of "Lost Socks" on detergent boxes?

Why do people point to their wrist when asking for the time, but don't point to their crotch when they ask where the bathroom is?

What's the difference between a magician and a large pizza?
The pizza can feed a family of four.

I usually don't brag about my finances but my credit card company calls me every week to tell me my balance is outstanding!

You know you are at a bad buffet when the carving table has Spam.

It is amazing how many weathermen get the forecast wrong but we still rely on a groundhog for the weather.

♪ ♪♪ "What would you do if I sang out of tune. Would you stand up and walk out....♪ ♪♪ ..Hey, where is everybody going?

I lost my job as a stage designer and I left without making a scene.

Green is my favorite color. I like it more than blue and yellow combined

A snail is returning home late at night and has to cut though a dark alley. As he is passing though, he is mugged by two slugs. Later on at the police station, the officer asks him, "Can you give me a description of the assailants?"
The snail ponders this for a moment and then replies, "Gee, I'm not sure... it all happened so fast."

Is reading "Do not touch" in braille breaking the rules?

Dear God, my prayer for this year is a FAT bank account and a THIN body. Please don't mix it up like you did this year.
New Year's Resolution: Option A, lose weight. Option B, buy larger clothes.

One Armed Waiters; They can take it but they can't dish it out.
No matter how old you are, an old used wrapping tube is still a light saber.

My phone just filmed a three hour documentary about life in my pocket.

Three out of four doctors surveyed think the fourth doctor doesn't know what he is talking about.

If first you don't succeed, quit. No sense making a fool of yourself.

Anyone who thinks that "Love is more important than money"
has clearly never tried paying off a loan shark with a cuddle!

Just watched The Lorena Bobbitt Story-
The Director's Cut
Too soon?

To the person who stole my glasses, I will find you, I have contacts.

The lady next door is stalking me. She keeps finding me hiding in her hedges.

New Medicare Dating App
Meet people with the same illness to share medications

I had to stop doing fish jokes but they never really cod on.

Just got back from the gym and some idiot on the treadmill next to me had a bottle of water in the Pringles can holder.

Telling a person to "Calm down" really never goes over very well.

I decorated our apartment with pictures of small dogs...
Wife was not happy and accused me of having an all terrier motif!
When Edison invented the light bulb, people thought it was just a filament of his imagination.

Turkeys cannot speak, so they usually take their secrets to the gravy.

Every psychic I visit is either really angry or really sad.
I'd like to find a happy medium.

A midget fortune teller escaped from prison, headlines read "SMALL MEDIUM at LARGE!"

Husband: Lets go out tonight and have a good time.
Wife: Great! If you get home before me, leave the key under the mat.

I am so old that I was the waiter at The Last Supper....and they wanted separate checks.

Church Bulletin:
The class on prophecy has been cancelled due to unforeseen circumstances

Q: How do Mexicans slice their pizzas?
A: Little Caesars

Hippos are big, ugly and smell like pigs. Maybe I am being just a little hippocritical.

I'm at the age where I have to make a noise when I bend over. It's the law.

You are officially old when you can tell the weather with your knees.

The secret to a successful marriage is to marry the one who match your values, principles and thermostat settings.

My friend who has a bit of a stutter was telling us about his Nanna.
By the end of it we were all singing 'Hey Jude!'

So apparently, I've got this awful disease where I can't stop telling airport jokes. The doctor says it's terminal!

I really worked up a sweat at my twenty minute workout but I finally got my socks on.

If I make you breakfast in bed, a simple "thank you" is all I need. Not all this "how did you get in my house?!" business.

How long have I been working for this company?
Ever since they threatened to fire me.

Yesterday, I told my doctor that I was having some memory loss. He made me pay in advance.

Pole dancing at my age is really just holding onto the safety bar in my bathtub.

At my age, I am finding that gravity is my worst enemy.

Little known fact, before the invention of the crowbar.
Crows had to do their drinking at home.

Susie sells sea shells by the sea shore..where shells are free.Why didn't her parents point this out?

How did the universe get together to decide that mint was the flavor of a fresh mouth? We can't make a decision on anything else.

Tomorrow is National Jamaican Hairstyle Day!
I am already dreading it.

The first five days after the weekend are the hardest.

It would be really funny to find out that Chef Bobby Flay has a wife named Sue.

A beer in the hand is better than two in the fridge.

What do you call an exploding monkey?
A Baboom!

Fun Fact:
There are no canaries on Canary Islands. Same with the Virgin Islands. No canaries there either.

I was going to tell an animal joke but its irrelephant.

I've just been fired from the clock making factory after all those extra hours I put in. I don't look good naked.

My doctor hands me the gown and tells me to put it on over my clothes.

When I see a food that has 50% less fat, I think great!
I can eat twice as much now.

If I had to chase women at my age, it would have to be downhill

General Custer invented the Arrow shirt.
Too soon?

Burial charges are up! High cost of living is to blame.

I used to make belts out of watches. What a waist of time!

What do you call a waffle you drop in the desert?
San Diego.

What color is a window? Well, the answer's pretty clear.

Since water made her melt, the Wicked Witch of the West never took a bath.

I'd like to start dieting but I've got too much on my plate.

When does a joke become a dad joke?
When it becomes apparent.

I am at the age where if they light all my candles on my cake, the firefighters are put on high alert.

Poor? My mother would send me next door with a button and to ask our neighbor if she would sew a shirt on it.

A hypnotist used his watch to put 12 volunteers to sleep. He dropped his watch and said "Crap" The show was over!

Life is like an elevator...
It has its ups and downs but most of the time you just get the shaft.

I was once in a band called
'The Radiators'.
We were a warm up act.

An old Japanese gardener asked me what I
knew about bonsai trees.
I answered.."Very little."

My wife found out I was cheating after she
found the letters I was hiding. She's never
playing Scrabble with me again!

Never agree to plastic surgery if your
doctor's office is filled with Picasso
paintings.

When I was young, I used to go skinny
dipping. Now that I am old and fat, I go
chunky dunking.

If a magician asks if you want to see JUST one card effect, don't believe him. It's a trick.

Keep your dreams alive!
Hit the snooze button.

All this talk about artificial intelligence. Enough already, Washington DC has had it for years.

Politicians are like diapers. They should be changed regularly and for the same reasons.

Four out of five people suffer from diarrhea. Does that mean that one enjoys it?

New York City Travel Tip: The city does not employ "Wallet Inspectors"

An apple a day keeps the doctor away. I have a restraining order for throwing apples at my doctor.

You have the wrong lawyer if during your initial consultation he tries to sell you Amway products

You know you have a bad surgeon when you see an award on his wall from Hasbro for Best Operation Game Player.

Sign you have a bad lawyer:
He giggles every time he hears the word "Briefs"

I can sympathize with batteries.
I never get included in anything either.

If Russians pronounce B's as V's then
Soviet.

I was going to go to a seminar on how to be
more independent, but I had no one to go
with.

I didn't abandon my diet.
 I'm a desserter.

One bird can't make a pun.
But toucan.

I knew the mermaid was a math whiz
when I saw her algae bra

A garbage can is probably the hardest thing to throw away.

If you love someone, set them free. If they come back with the police, then you shouldn't have let them go.

Toilets are the only product that are number 1 and number 2 in the world!

It's so hot I saw a funeral procession pull through a Dairy Queen.

How many magicians does it take to pull a rabbit out of a hat?
One. It's a trick question.

IKEA stores would take forever to build if you were using only IKEA hardware and building materials.

Neil Armstrong told jokes about the moon landing but nobody laughed so he always said "Guess you had to be there!"

Let a smile be your umbrella and you will have a mouthful of rain.

When an octopus marriage breaks up, it's always the squids that suffer.

I'm hiding from exercise.
I'm in the Fitness Protection Program.

I got pulled over by the police.
Police: "Turn around"
Me: "Every now and then I get a little bit lonely and you're never coming round"
Police: "Turn around."
Me: "Bright eyes" It was then I got tasered.

Went to a Halloween Costume Contest dressed as a giraffe. I didn't win but at least I can hold my head up high.

There Is More Than One Way To Skin A Cat is not my favorite cookbook.

A student at a marketing school went up to a beautiful girl and gave her a big hug.
The girl said "what was that?"
The guy said "direct marketing"
The girl slapped his face.
Rubbing his cheek, he said "What the heck was that?" She said "Customer feedback!

My job is to drill holes in things and then bolt them together...It's boring and riveting at the same time.

I went to lunch with a champion chess player.
It took him 8 minutes to pass me the salt.

In a recent survey, California ranked #1 in both adultery and depression. It's a sad state of affairs.

A nine year old girl has disappeared after using moisturizer that makes you look ten years younger!

When I found out I was bipolar, I didn't know whether to laugh or to cry.

My wife told me that I twist everything she says to my advantage, so I took it as a compliment.

IT Guy "Have you tried disabling cookies?"
I said, "Well, I once bit the legs off a gingerbread man!"

It was my day to procrastinate but I will do it next week.

If at first you don't succeed, do it the way your wife asked you to do it in the first place.

When one door closes, another door opens...This damn IKEA cabinet!

Interviewer "So where do you see yourself in 15 years?"
Me:" my best trait is that I am a great listener."

My wife has some chiropractic magazines for sale.
She has a lot of back issues.

Duck walks into a bar... "Got any bread?" "No" "Got any bread?" "No" "Got any bread?" "No...and if you ask me again I'll nail your beak to the bar" "Got any nails?" "No" "Got any bread?"

The more I age, the more I need glasses. Glasses of wine, glasses of beer…

Haunted French pancakes always give me the crepes.

Humility is what really makes me awesome!

At the age where I have been there, done that! I just don't know remember where 'there' is or what I've 'done'

What do you call a sleepwalking nun?
A roamin' Catholic!

My wife just tripped and dropped a basket full of freshly ironed clothes... I just sat back and watched it all unfold!

I am at the age where I can cough, sneeze, fart and pee at the same time!

I have a chronic fear of giants…
Feefiphobia.

The man who invented barcodes walks into a bar, thin bar, thin bar, bar, thick bar, bar, thin bar, thin bar!

What kind of steps will I take if another earthquake happens.
Big Ones!

I met a drunk ventriloquist who said she wanted to sleep with me but I didn't know whether it was her or the beer talking.

My grandfather fought the Germans and my father fought the Koreans. My family couldn't get along with anybody.

You never need an item that has been in your house for 25 years until the day the garbage truck takes it away!

If you have a cold, instead of cough syrup, try 5 laxative tablets. It won't cure you of your cold but you will be afraid to cough.

Everybody is in awe of a lion tamer in a cage with half a dozen wild animals...everybody except a school bus driver.

Two guys came to my door while I was vacuuming. They wanted to watch me clean. Just what I needed...Je-Hoovers Witnesses!

News Flash: A cement mixer truck and a prison van collided. Passengers escaped. Police are looking for a few hardened criminals.

To keep cool, I like to strip down to my underwear and open the freezer door. Not allowed in Ralph's Market anymore.

I just can't seem to finish this woodworking project, but it's not for lacquer trying.

Two florists got married. It was an arranged marriage.

Wife and I decided to take a romantic vacation. She is going Thursday-Saturday. I am going Sunday-Wednesday.

Setting the temperature in our house is a compromise because I'm always cold and my wife is always hot, so I'm always cold.

I finally came up with a good defense for an argument I had with my wife in 2007.

Wife and I love teamwork! She tells me what to do and I do it! What a Team!

I went to the new Star Wars Sandwich Shop. I had the Ham Solo with a side of R-2Tofu and the Chewbaklava.

I told the salesman I couldn't make up my mind about a new mattress. I said "Let me sleep on it!"

Electricians have to strip to make ends meet.

Doctor: Do overweight people run in your family?
Me: Nobody runs in my family.

I've noticed that my Cheerios have been tasting different lately. I don't know why, I am still pouring the same beer on them.

Why do laxatives have a best before date on them?
What's the worst that could happen?

As I suspected, someone has been adding soil to my garden...
The plot thickens!

Holy Water Recipe:
Boil the Hell out of it

Even though The Beatles changed history, no one took them seriously when they suggested "Eight Days A Week"

You hired a bad contractor ...if on the day the insulation is to be put down, he shows up wearing a Pink Panther costume.

If you knock on a psychic's door and she asks "Who is it?"turn around and walk away.

I am at the age where a lifetime warranty on a product doesn't mean that much to me anymore.

I, for one, am a great fan of Roman numeral puns!

Summer is here so time to put on my lifeguard shirt, get my binoculars and head to the Nude Beach. No one has thrown me out yet.

Last night, I ate at a fancy restaurant. I had the roast parrot. It was good but it kept repeating on me.

I lent my friend $5,000 to have plastic surgery. Now I don't know what he looks like, so I can't get my money back!

Diet Day 1: Just got rid of all the fattening food in the house.
They were delicious!

Proud of myself today.
I went to the bathroom without my phone.

I once designed cul de sacs.
It was a dead end job.

How to answer the phone from a
Telemarketer:
"Ok, Jim, I buried the body...when are you
picking me up?"

Whenever I get handed a CVS receipt, in
my head, I hear the clerk say..."We killed a
tree...and now you are an accomplice"

Instead of saying, "And here's your
receipt," cashiers should say, "Will you
throw this away for me?"

I just had amnesia and déjà vu... I think
I've forgotten this before.

At the gym:
 Me: "What does this machine do?"
"Sir, that's a bench." Me: "Perfect."

I think I could make a fortune selling "No Soliciting" signs door to door.

I just saw an ad for a glass coffin company ....will it succeed?
Remains to be seen.

Coffee is a such a big deal that they named a table after it.

I just read a book about cooking using only one pan.
 It was called "Do You Have the Skillet Takes"

I did eight sit-ups this morning. That may not sound impressive, but you can only hit the snooze button so many times.

Had to put 4 bandages on my face today. I was putting on cologne when I got paper cuts from the magazine.

I can remember the words to all   the Beatles songs but I can't remember if I put down the garage door five minutes ago.

If your parachute doesn't open, you are jumping to a conclusion.
I was doing self checkout at Walmart and the manager came over and said that I could go on break.

I wanna stop eating cold turkey but I don't know how.

 I've won the Annual World's Best Liar award seven times this year!

A little birdie told me to see a shrink, which made sense since animals shouldn't be talking at all.

I don't like to cast aspersions, but it's the only way I get to use the word aspersions.

I just watched a play about the weather. There were about 20 actors playing clouds. I think it was overcast.

I got a huge weight off my shoulders today. My obese parrot died.

A weasel walks into a bar. The bartender says "Wow, I have never served a weasel before. What can I get you?"
"Pop" goes the weasel.

I am on the new garlic diet?
I didn't lose much weight, but from a distance, my friends think I look thinner.

I told my wife that the doctor told me to get a hot mama. She said "No dear, he said you have a heart murmur!"

A musical chord walks into a bar wanting to get a drink. The bartender says, "I'm sorry. I cannot serve you. You're A minor"

If you have a good remedy for clearing out ear wax, give me a shout!

A strange day today. First of all I found a hat full of money, then I was chased by an angry man with a guitar!

I have a FLAT stomach… the L is silent.

I needed a password eight characters long... So I picked Snow White and the Seven Dwarfs!

Watched a dog chase his tail and thought what a waste of time. Then I realized, I was watching the dog chase his tail.

To the people who are trying to overcome their paranoia, I'm behind you all the way.

How many South Americans does it take to change a light bulb? A Brazilion!

Always be nice to the person who is packing your parachute!

Plagiarism is getting into trouble for something you didn't do.

Did anyone see the joke I posted recently about my spine? It was about a weak back.

Apparently, when you go to donate blood it's supposed to be YOUR blood.

The way to stop bank robberies would be to put a Dunkin Donuts in every bank. That way the cops would already be there!

I joined a health club last year. It cost me $400. So far, I have lost 400 dollars.

The best salesman in the world is the guy who sells receipt paper and ink to CVS!

Don't ask me about my pan pizza, it's personal.

The Kleptomaniacs Society has been postponed this evening. Somebody stole the chairs.

I have loved my recliner for years. We go way back!

Last night, I went to the new Jewish Vegan Restaurant.
 It was called Soy Vey!

Mountains are funny. In fact, they are hill areas!

I have a fear of speed bumps but I am getting over it.

My wife bumped into a friend while we were grocery shopping so I spent the time completing an entire online course on Real Estate.

Millard Fillmore died after a long battle of trying to convince people he was once the President

What's big, gray, and makes you jump? The elephant of surprise.

I hate the key of E minor. It gives me the E-B-G-Bs.

Flatulence, n. Emergency vehicle that picks up someone who has been run over by a steamroller.

Lawrence Welk named his twin daughters Anna one Anna two.

My rude neighbor was banging on my door at 3 AM. Luckily, I was up practicing my drums so it didn't bother me.

I just read a book called How to make Tunnels. It was boring.

They should make a Segway that vacuums.

It now takes 45 seconds to scroll to my birth date. I am surprised when I find it is still there.

Love is blind and marriage is an eye opener.

Marriage isn't a word, it's a sentence.

A man is incomplete until he is married. Then he is finished.

There was an explosion at a French cheese factory.
 All that was left was de brie.

Wife: Do you want dinner?
Husband: Sure, what are my choices?
Wife: Yes and no.

Wife: Do you love me still?
Husband: I have never seen you that way.

My wife and I love being spontaneous as long as we plan it about a month in advance.

They dared me to jump off a cliff, but it was just a bluff.

Autocorrect isn't a big deal.
 Women had it before it was a computer thing.

A good wife always forgives her husband when she's wrong.

98% percent of the population is stupid. Luckily I'm part of the other 6%.

The secret to a great Hawaiian pizza is to cook it at aloha temperature.

Grocery shopping with my wife is fantastic. She saves us a ton of money by saying to me.
 "Put that back!"

I have over 1000 pictures of grocery items on my phone from texting my wife and saying "Is this what you want?"

Last night I drank 8 cans of Sprite and I burped 7 up! Magic, Poof!

My doctor wanted me to bend down and touch my toes.
I asked him if it was alright just to wave at them.

Wife: "I look fat. Can you give me a compliment?"
Husband: "You have perfect eyesight."

People ask us what is the secret of being married a long time. We just say that we are just to lazy to find somebody else.

A good limbo dancer lowers the bar for everyone else.

My dad suffered from short term memory loss.
I hope it doesn't run in the family because my dad had it too!

The guy who invented solitaire Taekwondo is probably kicking himself right now.

Knock knock
Who's there?
Yah.
Yah who?

When does bread rise?
When you yeast expect it.

Sent my DNA to Ancestry to have them look up my family tree. I found out I was the sap!

My dad told me to make little things count... So now I'm teaching math to a dwarf!

I failed my ventriloquist exams...
 I can't say I'm surprised!

I've cut down on my drinking and now only have one beer before going to bed... Last night I went to bed four times!

I dream of a world where chickens can cross the road without having their motives questioned!

It took me a long time to figure out I'm a slow learner

The female bartender at my local bar just got her nose pierced.
 I am really bad at darts

I had acupuncture today and now my voodoo doll walks with a limp.

I had an unemployed dwarf do a bit of casual work for me; he asked to be paid under the table.

People who don't know the difference between "burro" and "burrow" don't know their ass from a hole in the ground.

I think my neighbor is stalking me as she's been googling my name on her computer. I saw it through my telescope last night.

Arguing with your wife is like reading a software license agreement...
In the end, ignore it all and click, "I Agree.

conjunctivitis.com - a site for sore eyes!

I love jokes about eye doctors. The cornea the better.

So apparently you can't use "beef stew" as a password. It's not stronganoff.

Rejected Greeting Card:
 "As the days go by, I think of how lucky I am....that you're not here to ruin it for me."

You know you are addicted to the internet if you refer to going to the bathroom as downloading

Doctor put me on a diet.
He said it was OK to cheat once in awhile.
My wife won't like me dating other women even with a doctor note.

Signed up For Aerobics. They told me to wear loose fitting clothes...if I had any, I wouldn't have signed up for Aerobics.

Once again, I missed the deadline with my publisher about my book "Professional Procrastination" Maybe next year!

To the dude flipping me off for honking at him — your phone is on top of your car. If you die and come back as a hillbilly, it is called reintarnation.

Last night I stayed a night in the YMCA... It was really nice but I don't want to make a song and dance of it!

Once again, the Anti-Social Social Club has cancelled its meeting for this month.

This lady in Walmart was staring at me like she'd never seen someone spraying on deodorant and putting it back on the shelf.

The last thing I need is a burial plot

In 1969, a phone call was made from the White House to the moon. Today, I can't get my WiFi to work 20 feet from the router.

My friend thinks it's easier to deal with fractions than with decimals.
I think he's missing the point.

I like to call in sick to places I don't work. Tomorrow I'm getting written up at Wal-Mart and getting a week's suspension.

I feel heroic for giving blood everyday, but maybe I am just diluting myself.

I've never been good at scrap booking...
...but I guess I can give it the ol' collage try.

We didn't know what blood type my grandfather had so we had to say goodbye and even to the end he kept saying "Be Positive!"

Just seen a man slumped over a lawn mower crying his eyes out...
He said he'll be fine, he's just going through a rough patch!

Church notice: The Ladies Liturgy Society will meet. Mrs. Davis will sing "Put Me In My Little Bed" accompanied by the pastor. The man who invented Velcro has died. RIP

How do you know you've got a good tax accountant?
He's had a loophole named after him.

After my pet dolphin died, I felt like I didn't have a porpoise anymore.

I saw my neighbor talk to her cat like it understood what she was saying...when I told this to my dog...we just laughed.

If your wife doesn't shake her head and give you an eye roll, are you really married?

Thank goodness I went to a fortuneteller. She said that somebody was going to swindle me out of my money.

I love to go camping as long as there is a king size bed, free slot play and valet parking.

I am at the stage where I can't get along with anybody. Sad to say that even my imaginary friends aren't speaking to me now.

I'm a kleptomaniac.
I have to take something for it

One day I changed a light bulb, crossed the road and walked into a bar...
Then I realized my whole life was a joke!
They all laughed when I said I was going to start a business selling nitrous oxide.

New exercise equipment should come with a yard sale sign.

Men Fact:
Slapping a woman on the butt and saying "How about getting me a cold one' is never romantic.

Welcome to the Plastic Surgery Addicts group... I see a lot of new faces here today!

"How's the diet going?"
"Not so good, I had three eggs for breakfast."
"Scrambled, boiled or poached?"
"Cadburys!"

Robinson Crusoe had a four day work week. He had all his work done by Friday.

My yoga instructor wanted me to try some new positions. I told her that I wasn't bending over backwards just to please her.

A woman has the last word in any argument. Anything a man says after that is the beginning of a new argument.

If it weren't for marriage, men would spend their lives thinking they had no faults at all.

People who swim in the river in Paris are in Seine.

Husband "I did nothing wrong, and I promise never to do it again."

Why does the Norwegian navy have bar codes on the side of their ships?
So they can Scan da navy in.

I am almost at the age where I should see an archaeologist instead of a doctor.

Even though I don't have much hair left, my wife gave me a comb for a present. I said "Thanks, I'll never part with it"

Worst pickup line ever
"Does this hanky smell like chloroform to you?"

I think my wife is putting glue on my antique weapons collection.
She denies it but I'm sticking to my guns!

Rejected greeting Card:
As the days go by, I think of how lucky I am
That you're not here to ruin it for me.

Formal attire at my age is shoes with laces!

Wife: I just got back from the Beauty Parlor
Husband: They were closed?
He never saw the baseball bat coming.

I will never forget my grandfather's last words. "Are you holding the ladder"

I think I should go on a diet. My driver's license says "Picture continues on the other side."

I used to make terrible apocalypse puns, but armageddon better at it.

Rejected greeting card:
You had your bladder removed, you're on the mends.
Here's a bouquet of flowers
And a box of Depends.

Dilate: To live a long life.

I'm reading a book about WD40... It's non-friction!

I was going to buy a Delorean but I would only drive it from time to time.

Rejected greeting card:
If we were on a sinking ship with only one life jacket, I'd miss you heaps and think of you often."

I told my wife to embrace her mistakes...
So she gave me a hug.

I asked my grandmother how she's
enjoying her new stairlift...
She said, "It's driving me up the wall."

I am so old that when I went to school
there was no history class.

I am just about at the "we thought you
were dead"age.

Label on work gloves: "For best results, do
not leave at crime scene."

Optometrist Sign:"If You Don't See What
You're Looking For, You've Come To The
Right Place."

You know you have a bad doctor
when...the tongue depressors taste faintly
of Fudgesicles.

Warning label on a can of Fix-a-Flat: "Not to be used for breast augmentation."

New Book:I Lost My Balance by Eileen Dover and Paul Down.

Then: Stud Muffin
Now: Bran Muffin

Things you don't want to hear in surgery: "Oh, yeah? If you think you're so good, you do it!"

Book Title:
Songs from 'South Pacific' by Sam and Janet Evening

One DNA talking to another DNA:
"Do these genes make me look fat?"

Music Store Sign:
Gone Chopin
Back in a Minuet

I tried to get a job in a health club, but they said I wasn't fit for the job.

There are more horse's asses than there are horses.

A boy scout went around his neighborhood looking for a job...
"I'll pay you $20 to paint my porch," said one neighbor.
The scout agreed and went to work. A few hours later, the scout knocked on the neighbor's door and said, "I'm all finished, but your car is a Mercedes, not a Porsche."

A: Zucchini
Q: What kind of bathing suit do animals wear at the zoo?

A: Zebra
Q: What is 25 times bigger than an A bra?

I got my DNA results. My mother : Iceland
My father: Cuba
Me: Ice Cube

A friend said she did not understand
cloning...
I told her that makes two of us.

I was supposed to go to a nudist wedding
this winter but the bride got cold feet.

Then: Cops told me to slow down.
Now: Doctor tells me to slow down.

I am at the age where if I drop a pen on the
floor, I have to go buy a new pen.

My friends grand dad was run over by a
boat in Venice... I offered him my sincere
gondolences!

TSA warning:
When going through the screening process with your Chapstick...don't say "I have a balm"

On a scale of 1 to 10, how much do you hate people that use a scale system for everything?

Why do they call it a Nabisco delivery truck? It should be called Oreo SpeedWagon!

Florida has self driving cars. No wait..sorry..just seniors who can't see over the steering wheel.

Shin: a device for finding furniture in the dark.

The Internet is a weapon of mass distraction.

My wife's pet name for me is "Please Stop That."

The first rule of the husband club is…
Hold on a sec, let me ask my wife.

If your wife asks for a belt and matching bag for Valentine's Day, it isn't for the vacuum cleaner! Next time I will know better!

What's the difference between a $20 steak and a $55 steak?
 February 14th.

7-11 store flowers on Valentine's Day:
Show someone you care slightly more than not at all.

The average dwarf height is 3ft. That's a little gnome fact.

"An apple a day keeps the doctor away" doesn't work if you are trying to date his wife.

Ambition is a poor excuse for not having enough sense to be lazy.

Whoever put the word laughter in the word manslaughter should be tickled to death.

Stop internet scams!
Don't be a victim!!
 Send $9.99 to me for details

I wanted to do a TV show about me being the sexiest man alive but I don't have a title.
 My wife said
"How about He? Haw!'

Autocorrect makes me say things I didn't Nintendo.

Fact: God's first name is Andy!
...from that song "Andy walks with me, Andy talks to me, Andy tells me that I am his own.."

The only place where you put your money where your mouth is the dentist's office.

Cleavage is the only thing that you can look down on and approve of at the same time.

Filling a whoopee cushion with chocolate pudding adds a whole new dimension to the joke.

I don't want to brag but I just completed a jigsaw puzzle in one week and the box said 3 to 5 years.

What do we want?
A cure for obesity.
When do we want it?
 After lunch!

I just read this book about how they build large cruise ships.
 It's riveting!

The cross eyed teacher got fired.
 She couldn't control her pupils

I'm still sore from the gym.
I fell down in front of it on my way to get donuts.

I got mugged by six dwarfs last night... Not happy!

To keep myself from getting burned out, I exercise for two days and then take the next thirty years off.

Please stay away from marijuana..it can cause memory loss
or even worse, memory loss.

My wife is thinking about leaving me because she thinks I'm obsessed with astronomy... What planet is she on?

To the person who stole my antidepressants, I hope you're happy.

I accidentally wore a red shirt to Target and, long story short, I'm covering for Delores this weekend.

You know your lawyer is bad
when he picks the selection of jurors by "Duck, Duck, Goose"

Bad Children's Book:
Pop Goes The Weasel and Other Great Microwave Games.

I almost had a psychic girlfriend but she left me before we met.

You mention Botox these days and no one even raises an eyebrow.

Don't tell me nothing is impossible, I could do that every day.

Ladies Bible Study is at 10 AM. All ladies are invited to lunch right after the BS.

The longest sentence is "I do"

Sign you need a new lawyer:
When the prosecutor's team sees who your lawyer is, they high-five each other.

Congress: The opposite of progress.

Fission: What people in Mayberry did when they caught fish

Invited a Jehovah's Witness in my house. I said, "Tell me about your religion?" He said "Um...I never made it this far before"

Travel Tip:
Say no to anyone in South America
who wants you to deliver a suitcase filled
with sugar to their grandmother in Miami.

Sign you have a bad lawyer;
He places a "NO REFUNDS" sign on the
defense table.

I got the results back from my Ancestry
DNA test.
 It seems that my relatives were from
Gilligan's Island.

If Wile E. Coyote has enough money to by
all that Acme crap why doesn't he buy his
dinner?

What do people in China call their good plates?

This girl said she recognized me from the vegetarian club, but I'd never met herbivore.

Pope's Favorite songs:
Girls Just Want To Be Nuns
Sistine Candles
Wind Beneath My Vestments

Geometry:
What an acorn said when it grew up.

She said "How much do you love me?"
He heard "I did something today that you are not going to like."

If dust is out of control in your house, when people come over just explain "This is where Grandma wanted us to spread her ashes"

Terminal illness: Sick of waiting at the airport.

My first parachute jump today and I was terrified. This guy strapped himself to me and we jumped out.
As we plummeted he said, "So, how long have you been an instructor?"

Apple pie: $2.00 in Jamaica, $3.00 in the Bahamas, $3.50 in Aruba.
 Those are the pie rates of the Caribbean.

I spent the entire morning trying to count the steps on an escalator.

Viagra is like an amusement park ...a very long wait for a two minute ride.

The slang term "What's Shakin" means something entirely different in earthquake areas.

Bacteria: The back door of a cafeteria.

I am going to work like a dog today.
Dogs don't work, therefore, lay around all day is what I was going for.

Woke up early today because my dog farted out loud and startled me. Then I realized that we don't have a dog.

The circus is not in tents as it used to be so Clown College enrollment is way down.

Senior Tip: Take the right pills by putting them in different Disney Pez dispensers.

Nitrate:The price after sundown.

Avoidable:What a bullfighter tries to do.

Marriage is a two way street that most of the time only goes one way.

Diet Soda: A drink you buy at 7/11 to go with a one pound bag of peanut M&M's.

This morning I made sure my wife woke up with a big smile on her face...I'm not allowed Sharpies in the bedroom anymore.

Least known Marx Brother: Skid

Yoga:
An hour of your life where you basically try not to pass gas.

Never try to guess your wife's size. Just buy her anything marked 'petite' and hold on to the receipt.

We were so poor growing up that we had to go to KFC just to lick other people's fingers.

If your wife ever brings up the topic of getting you more life insurance, you can be darn sure she thought of killing you.

I am at the critical stages of life. I have to finally make a decision. A diet or new pants.

Illiterate? Write today for free help.
Little Known Fact: The Greek god Pan loved cooking utensils.

There is a fine line between a numerator and a denominator... only a fraction of people will find this joke funny.
I want abs...olutely all the pizza.

I asked 100 women what shampoo they prefer to use while taking a shower... They all replied, "How did you get in here?"

Went to see the doctor about my blocked ear. "Which ear is it?" he asked. "2019!" I replied.

My new years resolutions are:
1.   Stop making lists. D. Be more consistent. 7. Learn to count.

Burglar Alarm:
Perfect gift for the person who has everything.

You're not completely useless. You can always serve as a bad example.

What do you call a beautiful woman on the arm of a banjo player? A tattoo.

I entered 10 puns in a pun contest hoping one would win, but no pun in ten did.

I read that Pavlov got dogs to eat at the sound of a bell..so let me get this ... Oh, got to go, my microwave just beeped.

The Time Management seminar will be Thursday around six or sevenish.

" Do whatever you want to do, I really don't care"
 It's a trap. Returning my motorcycle!

Old Proverb: Some people are like blisters… they don't show up until the work is done.
Tennis players: Love meant nothing to them.

"New year, new me" is a fun thing to say while committing identity theft.

Worldly advice:Never see a proctologist on the same day you participate in a chili cook-off.

Caesarean section: High-rent area in Rome.

Accordion to the latest statistics, it is easy to put in a musical instrument in a sentence without people noticing it.

Calories: Tiny creatures that live in the closet and sew your clothes a little tighter every night.

Irony: Drawing trees on paper

Wife: "Want to split a Christmas cookie? husband: By cookie, you mean the whole tin of them, right?

I am opening a new restaurant called Karma. No menu. You get what you deserve.

I went to a tough school. How tough was it? We even had our own coroner

I dated a female pirate but we broke up because she said I had a sunken chest and no booty.

I tried to get a job at the moisturizer factory. They said I should apply daily.

My dog once retrieved a stick from a mile away, I know it sounds far fetched.

I named my dog Five Miles so I could tell people I walked Five Miles every day.

At my age I am good at multi-tasking. I can laugh, cough, sneeze, fart and pee all at the same time.

I, put commas, in, weird places, so that, you, will, read, this, like William, Shatner.

My Mom used to say that a way to a man's heart is through his stomach....and that is how she lost her job as a surgeon.

Going to the barber is getting faster. Once he cuts my nose hairs, my eyebrows and my ear hairs, I'm done.

I just saw the license plate "BAA BAA" on a black jeep.

What do you call a fat psychic?
A four-chin teller!

Today I saw a dwarf prisoner climbing down the wall...I thought to myself, that's a little condescending

Why is it the longer I stay at home, the more homeless I look?

My New Year's Resolution is to get my friends to gain 15 pounds so I won't look so fat.

New Year's Resolution:
I will do less laundry and use more deodorant.

I was driving and hit a magician.
I mean, he came out of nowhere.

My favorite mythical creature? The honest politician.

Phone rings while the couple is in bed. The husband answers the phone "Hello? What? How the hell should I know? It's 200 miles away! Then he hangs up. Wife asks "Who was that? Husband says "Some jackass wanted to know if the coast was clear"

'I went to the zoo the other day, there was only one dog in it, it was a shitzu.'

I need to quit my job as a personal trainer because I'm not big enough or strong enough. I've just handed in my too weak notice.

Compromise: An amiable arrangement between husband and wife whereby they agree to let her have her own way.

If you have a parrot and you don't teach it to say, "Help, they've turned me into a parrot! You're wasting everybody's time.

My wife has left me because I'm too insecure…No wait, she's back. She just went to make a cup of coffee.

I hate it when people don't know the difference between your and you're…There so stupid.

How many ants need to be in your house before you can charge them rent? Ten!

Every morning, I tell my wife I am going for a jog but I don't go. It's a running joke.

My friends asked me to go camping, so I made a list of things I needed. 1. New Friends

Star Wars Trivia: Yoda's last name was Layheehoo.

My seminar on "How to Avoid Scams" has been cancelled. Tickets are non-refundable

Life Tip: Save thousands of dollars on buying new clothes by not going on a diet!

I don't eat any food that says it might kill me. Am I right, Artichoke?

I want to give a big shout out to everybody who is hard of hearing.

My superpower is that I can look my wife directly in the face for 10 minutes straight and not hear a single word.

Pronouncing words correctly is just not my fort.

The guy who stole my Diary died today, my thoughts are with his family.

People used to laugh at me when I would say "I want to be a comedian." Well nobody's laughing now

I was going to start Fish Pun today but I think I will scale back. If you have one, let minnow.

Uber and Lyft are exactly what our parents told us not to do when we were children.

No matter what I do, I cannot lose this 18 pounds... I mean I have tried everything short of diet and exercise.

Doing a little Christmas shopping, I am trying to find a Dollar Store with a layaway department

If you're behind someone at an ATM machine, let them know you're not a threat by gently kissing their neck.

Bad investment deal: Self Service Massage Parlor

I just met Stan Lee's vegan brother… Brocco!

I just met Bruce Lee's less attractive brother and sister, Ug and Home!

My retirement plan is a slippery floor at a McDonald's restaurant.

You do not have to report a Crackerjack prize as income on your taxes.

I think the kids enjoyed Trick or Treating at my house this year. Each kid got a 20% off coupon from Bed, Bath and Beyond.

There is still a chance that I will use my remote control Whoopie Cushion before I die. If I don't, I told my wife to put in my coffin.

A rooster walks into a bar. "What will you have? asked the bartender. Rooster says "Coca Cola'll do"

Marriage is like taking a bath… after you've been in it for a while, it isn't so hot.

FOR SALE: Braille dictionary. Must see to appreciate!

Words are powerful, so choose them good.

Odd Fact: Raymond Burr's son Tim worked as a lumberjack.

Free guitar, no strings attached.

I made alphabet soup with a laxative! Calling it "Letter Rip"

I tried to visit the inventor of toothpaste's house, but sadly, there was no plaque on it.

My neighbor's diary says that I have boundary issues.

A: Hickory Dickory Dock. Q: Who do you go to when you have a pain in your hickory dickory?

At my age, "Getting a little action" means I don't have to take any fiber today.

People I know are running marathons. Meanwhile, I am watching a show I don't like because the remote is out of reach.

I'm not bragging but my credit card company calls me every day to say my balance is outstanding.

I am having a "Stop being Gullible" seminar next Wednesday. Send $100 to me in a cashier check by next Tuesday.

Do these protons make my mass look big?

The man who created the anagram passed away today.
 "Erect a penis"

Sold my homing pigeon again on eBay.

The best advice I ever got was,"Don't let Sean Connery teach your dog to sit!"

A piranha can eat a child down to the bone in less than a minute.
 In other news, I lost my job at the aquarium today.

CLASSIFIED: An unexpected vacancy for a knife-thrower's assistant. Rehearsals start immediately.

I have a Polish friend who is a sound engineer. I have a Czech one too.

What do you call a Frenchman wearing sandals?
Phillipe Phillope.

Husband: " It is important to get your breasts examined twice a year"

Wife: "First of all, you are not a doctor and second, you are going to get us kicked out of Trader Joe's"

Woke up this morning, looked down and one of my toes was missing .

There was a note stuck to my foot that said, 'Gone To Market'

How do you tell the gender of an ant?
Put it in a glass of water.
If it sinks its a girl ant.
If it floats its buoyant.

I did a push up today, well actually I fell so I had to use my hands to get back up so, close enough.

I see that we are almost out of shampoo, conditioner, body lotion and small bars of soap. Time to book another hotel stay.

Ever notice how loud the sound of opening a beer can at work is?

My bank just called me about suspicious activity on my account... They didn't believe I bought a gym membership.

My wife says she's going to leave me because of my poker addiction... I think she's bluffing!

I ran five miles today.. Finally, I had to say, "OK Lady, here's your purse back…

When an escaped prisoner was caught camping out in the woods it was a clear case of criminal in tent.

How do you know your old? People call at 8 p.m. and ask, "Did I wake you?"

Saw a woman wearing the word Guess on her jeans. So I took a chance and said "240?"
 I will be out of hospital later today.

The ESP club meeting has been cancelled for this evening. The next meeting will be on....

I will be posting telepathically today. So if you think of something funny, that was me.

I can't remember what 51, 6 and 500 are in Roman numerals.
 I'm LIVID!

If you had to decide between a diet and a piece of chocolate, would you prefer dark, white or milk chocolate?

I saw my wife, slightly tipsy, yelling at the TV: "Don't go in there! Don't go in the church, you idiot!"
She's watching our wedding video again!

So apparently RSVP'ing back to a wedding invite 'maybe next time' isn't the correct response.

I just read in the newspaper about the dangers of drinking alcohol. So that is it! I am giving it up. No more reading for me!

A beautiful woman came up to me today and called me a real looker!
Well...she said Peeping Tom but I know what she meant!

Please keep me in your thoughts and prayers right now. Nothing is going on, I'm just a narcissist.

I'm on a whisky diet. I've lost three days already.

You know you're old if your walker has an airbag.

You know you're getting old when bending over is a one-way trip.

I ordered 2000 lbs. of Chinese soup. It was Won Ton.

Outvoted 1-1 by my wife again.

What do cannibals do at a wedding? Toast the bride and groom.

This is nuts. I bought the Where's Waldo movie and now I can't find it.

People ask me what time I go to bed. Usually about three hours after I fall asleep on the couch.

Don't you hate it when someone answers their own questions?
I do.

I used to be in a band, we were called 'lost dog'.
You probably saw our posters.

I just saved a bundle on home security by not having any stuff worth stealing.

60% of being an adult is repeatedly walking to the refrigerator to see that there's nothing in there to eat.

I finally found a Psychic who knows how I like my steaks.
 She is a rare medium! Well Done!

There is some person waiting at the plastic company just waiting to say the words "Well, that's the last straw"

My health care coverage is so bad that my primary care doctor is Web MD.

It finally happened.
The iron in my blood has turned to lead in my pants

I took the shell off my racing snail to see if it would go faster but it only made him sluggish.

I'm currently boycotting any company that sells items I can't afford.

My wife's mad at me again. She was up for making a sex movie last night and all I did was suggest we should hold auditions for her part.

I recently took up meditation.
It beats sitting around doing nothing.

Anyone know how to get a financial advisor to stop laughing?

Getting paid to sleep would be my dream job.

I had a few drinks last night at a bar so I took a bus home. I never drove one before.

I hope when I inevitably choke to death on Swedish Fish people just say I was killed by sharks and leave it at that.

Marriage is nature's way of preventing people from fighting with strangers.

Someone ripped some pages out of both ends of my dictionary today so now, it just goes from bad to worse.

Some idiot asked my wife
 "Why is dinner taking so long?" and now I am sitting on the porch without dinner posting on Facebook.

Eye jokes, the cornea, the better.
I think I still have it. There is a girl at the grocery store that is always checking me out.

If you think your job is boring, try mine as an Amish electrician.

Just burned 2,000 calories. That's the last time I leave brownies in the oven while I nap.

The only exercise I get these days is when I jog my memory.

I didn't think these new orthopedic shoes would help me at all but I stand corrected.

I explained to my 4-year-old grand daughter that it's perfectly normal to accidentally poop your pants..
but she's still making fun of me.

Father: "Son, you were adopted."
Son: "What?! I knew it! I want to meet my biological parents!"
Father: "We are your biological parents. Now pack up, the new ones will pick you up in 20 minutes."

A wife chewed out her husband "Doesn't it embarrass you that people have seen you go up to the buffet table five times?"
"Not a bit," the husband replied. "I just tell them I'm filling up the plate for you."

I have to start dressing better.
I went for a walk today and four people offered to take me to a shelter and get me some food

An auction is a place where if you sneeze you can accidentally end up with a $15k lamp.
Unrelated ... For Sale, 1 Lamp $15k OBO.

"Maybe if I gotten a World's Best Dad shirt, I wouldn't be this mad" Darth Vader

What was St. Joesph's last name? Aspirin

Most of the calories I burn at the gym are from pulling out my wedgie.

If you have broken ribs,
laughter might not be the best medicine.

I wish they would put a gym in the liquor store so I could lift my spirits

I bought a new deodorant stick today. The instructions read: REMOVE WRAPPER AND PUSH UP BOTTOM. I can hardly walk now, but whenever I have gas, the room smells divine.

Things not to say when you are on a job interview.
"You want the rest of this beer?"

Not to brag, but I finally finished that bottle of Worcestershire sauce I bought in 1978.

Marriage secret
You should argue with your wife only when she's not around.

The seven ages of man: spills, drills, thrills, bills, ills, pills and wills.

Feeling kind of proud today. I lifted almost 200 pounds.
 I fell down and got back up again.

If you show up late for a cannibal dinner party, you will probably get the cold shoulder.

I really hate to do this but tomorrow I have to tell several highways that they are adopted.

Little known fact:
Darth Vader's first wife was named Ella.

My wife said that if she won the lottery, she would still love me.
She would miss me but she would still love me.

Ask me about my vow of silence.

"I will race you to the bathroom"
I quietly say to my bladder.

The last layer of skin on the roof of my
mouth finally grew back from that Hot
Pocket I ate in 2009.

How do you get a magician to show you a
hundred card tricks?
Ask him to show you one.

It's amazing how one housefly can undo all
those anger management sessions I had.

I guess I am old. I was digging through my
childhood items and I found my
autographed copy of the Bible.

I'm reading a book about how to levitate. I can't put it down.

I am reading a horror novel in braille, something bad is going to happen, I can feel it!

I ordered a chicken and an egg from Amazon. Now I wait!

When a chickpea gets killed it is called hummuscide.

My wife says I have two faults.
 I don't listen, and something else!

Got a wonderful letter from Jennifer Lopez today. Well, it was a restraining order but at least she is thinking about me.

I want to open a cigar shop near the Vatican.
 Calling it Holy Smokes!

I've learned that life is like a roll of toilet paper. The closer it gets to the end, the faster it goes.

Signed up for an exercise class and the guy said "How flexible are you? I said "I can't make Tuesdays"

I just cross-bred a crocodile and a homing pigeon... I expect that'll come back to bite me!

A doctor says to his patient, "I have bad news and worse news"."Oh dear, what's the bad news?" asks the patient.The doctor replies, "You only have 24 hours to live.""That's terrible", said the patient.

"How can the news possibly be worse?"The doctor replies, "I've been trying to contact you since yesterday."

You want to have some fun? Start a fight with your wife when she has the hiccups.

An ink drop was crying because his mother was in the pen doing a long sentence.

I just got a talking scale. It keeps saying "one at a time, please"

I went to an antique auction today. Three people bid on me.

My neighbor knocked on my door at 2:30 this morning. Luckily for him I was still up playing my bagpipes.

I'm writing a book about reverse psychology.
Please don't buy it.

I don't want to make anyone jealous, but I can still fit into the socks I wore in high school.

My father invented the side car mirror. I won't get any royalties because we're not as close as we appear.

My seminar
"How to avoid frauds"
is canceled.
Tickets are non-refundable.

You can tell a lot about a woman's mood just by her hands.
 If they are holding a gun, she's probably upset.

The hardest part of dating a blind woman
is getting her husband's voice right.

I am going to keep following my dreams
until they file a restraining order.

I am only two steps away from being a
vegetarian. Cows eat grass. I eat cows.

She said to me "Nothing would make her
happier than a diamond necklace."
So I bought her nothing.

I try to live every day as though it were my
last and who wants to do laundry on the
last day they're alive?

Live each day as if it was your last…and
someday you will be right.

I've been told I'm condescending
(that means I talk down to people)

Roses are red, violets are blue, I'm schizophrenic and so am I.

Watching a report of a woman getting only 7 years for killing her husband, wife says "You mean, I would have been out by now?"

People always say "It's neither here nor there"
 Then where the Hell is it?

I always wanted to be a Gregorian monk, but I never got the chants.

I once gave my seat to a blind lady. That is how I got fired as a bus driver.

I saw a lizard telling some great jokes. He was a stand up chameleon.

A man comes home and yells joyfully:
"Honey I won the Lotto! Pack your things for a nice big vacation!"
She asks: "Awesome! Should I pack for warm or cold weather?"
Man beams: "I don't care. Just be out in a hour."

Hey Honey, what do you say to a nice walk?
Oh Harry, that would be lovely!
Wonderful. Could you bring me some beer and cigarettes on your way back?

December is the month when the kids begin to discuss what to get Dad for Christmas.
Some insist on a shirt.
Others insist on a pair of socks
The argument always ends in a tie.

Times are tough these days. I saw a guy kicking a can down the street. I asked what he was doing. He said "Moving"

A man finds a snail on his porch. He picks it up and hurls it in the street.
A year later, the man finds the same snail on the porch. The snail says "What the hell was that all about?"

The inventor of throat lozenges has died and there will be no coffin at his funeral.

People ask me if I have empathy.
 I don't know and I don't care

Auto correct has become my worst enema.

"So how was that pill I gave you for your love life?" the doctor asked.

"Great, I took one just before we had dinner. It worked like a charm. My wife and I were eating our meal when the pill started to work its magic. We didn't even finish our meal. We had the best time ever right there at the table. I have to thank you Doctor! "

"Great....any side effects?"

"Well...just one. We are not allowed in Denny's anymore."

Just before the funeral services, the undertaker came up to the very elderly widow and asked,

'How old was your husband?'

'98,' she replied, 'Two years older than me'

'So you're 96,' the undertaker commented.

She responded , 'Hardly worth going home, is it?

An elderly couple are in church. The wife leans over and whispers to her husband, "I just let out a long, silent fart. What should I do?" The husband replies, "First off, replace the batteries in your hearing aid!

Walmart Fun: Go to housewares and set all the alarm clocks to go off in five minute intervals!

I stayed at a great hotel in Las Vegas. The towels were so big and fluffy I could hardly close my suitcase.

During a recent vacation in Las Vegas, a man went to see a popular magic show. After one especially amazing feat, a man from the back of the theater yelled, "How'd you do that?" "I could tell you, sir", the magician answered, "But then I'd have to kill you." After a short pause, the man yelled back, "OK, then... just tell my wife!"

A man had been drinking at the bar for hours when he mentioned something about his girlfriend being out in the car. The bartender, concerned because it was so cold, went to check on her. When he looked inside the car, he saw the man's friend, Dave, and his girlfriend kissing one another. The bartender shook his head and walked back inside. He told the drunk that he thought it might be a good idea to check on his girlfriend. The fellow staggered outside to the car, saw his buddy and his girlfriend kissing, then walked back into the bar laughing.

"What's so funny?" the bartender asked.

"That stupid Dave!" the fellow chortled, "He's so drunk, he thinks he's me!"

A wife comes home late one night and quietly opens the door to her bedroom. From under the blanket, she sees four legs instead of just her husband's two. She reaches for a baseball bat and starts hitting the blanket as hard as she can. Once she's done, she goes to the kitchen to have a drink. As she enters, she sees her husband there, reading a magazine. He says, "Hi darling, your parents have come to visit us, so I let them stay in our bedroom. Did you say hello?"

A wife got so mad at her husband she packed his bags and told him to get out. As he walked to the door she yelled, "I hope you die a long, slow, painful death." He turned around and said, "So, you want me to stay?"

A man and his wife were traveling down the highway when they saw the lights of a patrol car behind them. When they pulled over, the patrol man came up to the window and said, "I am going to give you two tickets. One because you were speeding and one because you didn't have your seat belt fastened." The man said, "I did too have my seat belt fastened. I just loosened it when you came up to the car." The Patrol Man said to the man's wife, "I know he didn't have his seatbelt fastened. Isn't that right, lady?" She replied, "Well, officer. I learned a long time ago not to argue with my husband when he's drunk."

A man comes home to find his wife of 10 years packing her bags. "Where are you going?" demands the surprised husband. "To Las Vegas! I found out that there are men that will pay me $500 cash to do what I do for you for free!" The man pondered that thought for a moment, and then began packing his bags. "What do you think you are doing?" she screamed. "I'm going to Las Vegas with you... I want to see how you're going to live on $1,000 a year!"

Once there was a snail who was tired of being slow. He went out and bought a really fast sports car and had the dealer paint a big 'S' on each side of it. Whenever someone saw him zooming past in his new car, they would say, "Hey, look at that S-car go!"

An old man lies on his death bed. He smells cooking from the kitchen by his wife of 50 years. He crawls to her, hauls himself up and grabs for a warm cookie.

His wife turns round and smacks him on the knuckles with a wooden spoon.

"They're for your funeral!" she shouted.

A kid was crying standing outside his house. A passer by asked: "Why are you crying?" Kid: "My parents are fighting inside the house." Passer by: "Who is your father?" Kid: "That is what the fight is about."

Statistically, six out of seven dwarfs are not Happy.

Three drunk guys entered a taxi. The taxi driver knew that they were drunk so he started the engine & turned it off again. Then said, "We have reached your destination". The 1st guy gave him money & the 2nd guy said "Thank you". The 3rd guy slapped the driver. The driver was shocked thinking the 3rd drunk knew what he did. But then he asked "What was that for?". The 3rd guy replied, "Control your speed next time, you nearly killed us!"

An Irish priest is driving down to New York and gets stopped for speeding in Connecticut. The state trooper smells alcohol on the priest's breath and then sees an empty wine bottle on the floor of the car. He says, "Sir, have you been drinking?" "Just water," says the priest. The trooper says, "Then why do I smell wine?" The priest looks at the bottle and says, "Good Lord! He's done it again!"

We walked past a swanky new restaurant in town.
"Did you smell that food?" she asked.
"It smells absolutely incredible!"
Being the kindhearted guy that I am, I thought what the hell, I'll treat her...
So I walked her past it again!

A guy joins a monastery and takes a vow of silence: he's allowed to say two words every seven years. After the first seven years, the elders bring him in and ask for his two words. "Cold floors," he says. They nod and send him away. Seven more years pass. They bring him back in and ask for his two words. He clears his throats and says, "Bad food." They nod and send him away. Seven more years pass. They bring him in for his two words. "I quit," he says. "That's not surprising," the elders say. "You've done nothing but complain since you got here."

The difference between Election day and Thanksgiving day. On Thanksgiving, you only get a turkey for the day.

"Poor Old fool," thought the well-dressed gentleman as he watched an old man fish in a puddle outside a bar. So he invited the old man inside for a drink. As they sipped their whiskeys, the gentleman thought he'd humor the old man and asked, "So how many have you caught today?"
The old man replied, "You're the eighth."

Husband: I am getting a motorcycle for $8,000 with extras for $2,000!
Wife: You don't need the extras.
Husband: Why?
Wife: Cause you're not getting a motorcycle!

A guy is reading his paper when his wife walks up behind him and smacks him on the back of the head with a frying pan. He asks, "What was that for?" She says, "I found a piece of paper in your pocket with Betty Sue written on it." He says, "Jeez, honey, remember last week when I went to the track? Betty Sue was the name of the horse I went there to bet on." She shrugs and walks away. Three days later he is reading his paper when she walks up behind him and smacks him on the back of the head again with the frying pan. He asks, "What was that for?" She answers, "Your horse called."

I need to put a small terrier up for adoption. The dog is really smart and barks a lot. If you interested, let me know and I will hop over the neighbor's fence and get it for you.

Sad news at the Nestle factory today when a member of staff was seriously injured when a pallet of chocolate fell more than 50 feet and pinned him underneath... He tried in vain to attract attention but every time he shouted "The Milky Way bars are on me" everyone cheered.

You can tell an ant's gender by putting it in water. If it sinks, girl ant. If it floats, buoyant.

A couple of hunters are out in the woods when one of them falls to the ground. He doesn't seem to be breathing and his eyes have rolled back in his head. The other guy whips out his mobile phone and calls the emergency services. He gasps to the operator: "My friend is dead! What can I do?" The operator, in a soothing voice, says: "Just take it easy. I can help. First, let's make sure he's dead." There is a silence, then a shot is heard. The guy's voice comes back on the line. He says: "OK, now what?"

FOR SALE BY OWNER – Complete set of Encyclopedia Britannica. 45 volumes. Excellent condition.$1,000.00 or best offer. No longer needed. Got married last weekend. Wife knows everything.

I recently added squats to my workouts by moving the beer into the bottom shelf of the fridge.

I had a dream that my wife got me really upset and mad.When I woke up I mentioned it to her and she said it was probably something I did wrong. So I had to apologize and take her to dinner.

A husband and wife are sitting at a table at his 50th high school reunion, and the husband keeps staring at a drunken woman sitting alone at a nearby table, downing glass after glass.
"Do you know her?" the wife asks.
"Yes," the husband says, with a self-important sigh. "She was my old girlfriend. I hear she took to drinking right after we split up those many years ago, and she hasn't been sober since."
"Wow!" the wife says. "Who would think a person could keep celebrating that long?"

80-year old Bessie bursts into the rec room at the retirement home. She holds her clenched fist in the air and announces, "Anyone who can guess what's in my hand can have sex with me tonight!"

An elderly gentleman in the rear shouts out, "An elephant?" Bessie thinks a minute and says, "Close enough."

A funeral service is held for a woman who just passed away. As the pallbearers carry the casket out, they accidentally bump into a wall. They hear a faint moan. They open the casket and find that the woman is actually alive. She lives for 10 more years and then dies. They have another funeral for her. At the end of the service, the pallbearers carry out the casket. As they are walking, the husband cries out, "Watch out for the wall!"

A juggler is sent to hell for his sins.
As he is being taken to his place of eternal torment, he sees a magician doing card tricks for a couple of beautiful woman.
"What a rip-off," the juggler muttered. I have to roast for all of eternity, and that magician gets to spend his time doing card tricks for beautiful women!"
Jabbing the juggler with his pitchfork, Satan snarled: "Who are you to question these women's punishment?"

The first rule of cleaning while listening to music is the toilet brush is never the microphone.

Did you ever get halfway though eating a horse and think, "I'm not as hungry as I thought I was."

Bob asked, "Have you ever cheated on me?"

Nancy replied, "Yes, three times."

"What?!", yelled Bob, "When?"

Nancy said, "Remember when the septic tank flooded back in '69 and we couldn't afford to fix it? I convinced the plumber to fix it for free."

"And?"

Nancy said, "Remember when you needed heart surgery in '75 and we didn't have insurance? I had the doctor treat you for free."

"And the third time?

"Do you remember when you ran for mayor back in '89 and you were behind by 200 votes…"

An old woman was arrested for shoplifting at a grocery store. When she appeared before the judge, the judge asked what she had taken. The lady replied, "A can of peaches." The judge then asked why she had done it. She replied, "I was hungry and forgot to bring any cash to the store." The judge asked how many peaches were in the can. She replied, "Nine." The judge said, "Well then, I'm going to give you nine days in jail--one day for each peach." As the judge was about to drop his gavel, the lady's husband raised his hand and asked if he might speak. The judge said, "Yes, what do you have to add?" The husband said, "Your honor, she also stole a can of peas."

A man walked into work on Monday with a two black eyes. His boss asked what happened.

The man said, "I was sitting behind a big woman at church. When we stood up to sing hymns, I noticed that her dress was caught in her crack, so I pulled it out. She turned around and punched me in the eye."

"Where did you get the second black eye?" the boss asked.

"Well," the man said, "I figured she didn't want it out, so I pushed it back in."

Last week a man knocked on my door and asked for a small donation towards the local swimming pool. I gave him a glass of water.

And in the words of Soupy Sales "Be true to your teeth and they won't be false to you"

If you want more entertainment, join Bob Carroll's Youtube Channel and watch Magic Monday. It's a tribute to magic and variety acts from around the world.

Magic Monday on Facebook-Youtube-Vimeo.

Made in United States
Orlando, FL
17 December 2024